hello

goodbye

ok

please

thank you

sit

stand up

work

finish

run

walk

drink

water

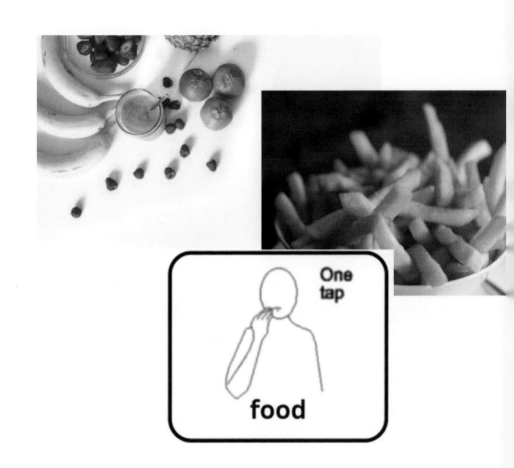

One
tap

food

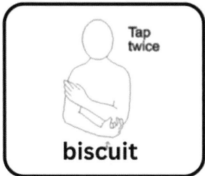

Tap
twice

biscuit

juice

Mime washing
hands

washing hands

happy

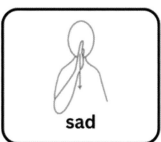

sad

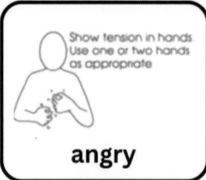

Show tension in hands.
Use one or two hands
as appropriate

angry

excited

frightened

love

The End

Printed in Great Britain
by Amazon